Paleo Bread: Easy and Delicious Gluten-Free Bread Recipes

by Aimee Anderson

This book contains material protected under International and Federal Copyright Laws and Treaties. Any unauthorized reprint or use of this material is prohibited. No part of this book may be reproduced or transmitted in any form or by any means, electronic or mechanical, including photocopying, recording, or by any information storage and retrieval system without express written permission from the author.

© 2013. All rights reserved.

Disclaimer:

This book is for entertainment purposes only. The publisher and author of this book are not responsible for any damages arising directly or indirectly from use of the information in this book. Use this information at your own risk. The publisher and author disclaim any liabilities for damages caused by use of the information contained herein.

None of the claims in this book should be construed as medical advice. Consult with a medical professional prior to making any changes in your life that could impact your health.

Contents

Introduction 6

The Paleo Diet: Going Caveman 8

What is Gluten? 11

Is Gluten Bad? 13

    Gluten Intolerance 14

    Celiac Disease 15

Identifying Foods that Have Gluten 18

Gluten and the Paleo Diet 23

Homemade Ingredients 25

    Almond Milk and Almond Flour 26

    Almond Butter 29

    Almond Meal 31

    Cashew Butter 33

    Coconut Milk and Coconut Flour 34

    Coconut Cream 37

    Coconut Oil 38

    Citrus Zest 41

Sweet Paleo Breads 42

    Almond Butter Bread 43

    Apple Cinnamon Nut Bread 45

    Banana Bread 48

    Blueberry Lemon Nut Bread 50

- Carrot Cake 53
- Cinnamon Bread 55
- Cranberry Bread 58
- Fruitcake 61
- Lemon Poppy Seed bread 64
- Pecan Raisin Bread 67
- Strawberry Shortcake 69
- Sweet Potato Bread 72
- Zucchini Bread 74

Traditional-Style Paleo Breads 77
- Almond Meal Pancakes 78
- Simple Paleo Bagels 80
- Cashew Butter Toast Bread 82
- Chestnut Bread 84
- Coconut Bread 86
- Flaxseed Bread 88
- Garlic Herb Bread 90
- Hamburger Buns 92
- Microwave Quick Bread 94
- Paleo Seed and Nut Loaf 96
- Pizza Crust 99
- Sandwich Bread 101

Rolls and Muffins 104
- Blueberry Breakfast Rolls 105

Banana Bread Breakfast Muffins 107

Dinner Rolls 109

Microwave Coconut Flour Muffins 111

Peach Muffins 113

Strawberry Muffins 115

Tapioca Flour Dinner Rolls 118

Additional Reading 120

Introduction

There are two types of people who are going to benefit from the information this book—those on a gluten-free diet and those who are Paleo dieters. If you aren't a Paleo dieter, don't let the fact that I've attached the name "Paleo" to this book scare you off. Yes, us Paleo dieters do eat like cavemen, but we're really not that much different from other gluten-free eaters.

We prefer to eat all-natural, healthy food that's free of chemicals and isn't processed. Doesn't sound too bad, does it?

Well, one of the foods that is eliminated from the Paleo diet is cereal grains, primarily because of the gluten content. That means traditional breads and most baked goods are off the table for the Paleo eater, as they are for others who are on a gluten-free diet.

A quick glance at the foods people consume around the globe reveals most cultures consume some form of bread made from cereal grains. It would be easy to make the assumption that cereal grains have been a part of our diet since man first started walking the Earth, but that assumption would be wrong. In fact, they've only been a part of our diet for such a short time they're barely a blip on the evolutionary radar.

For this reason, it's estimated a large portion of the population has at least minor problems when it comes to digesting the gluten found in cereal grains. It's tough to say just how bad the problem is because there's no easy way to identify most gluten sensitivities. If you suspect you're sensitive to gluten, discuss it with your physician to see if he or she recommends going gluten-free for a while to see if any health problems you're having subside.

If they do, you'll know gluten was a likely culprit and can take steps to eliminate it from your diet.

The Paleo Diet: Going Caveman

If you're new to the Paleo diet, here's a quick rundown of the tenets of going "Paleo."

Paleo dieters only eat the foods cavemen would have had access to in the Paleolithic era. These foods are the foods our bodies were designed by nature to consume. Evolution designed us in a specific way and our bodies are built to consume and process specific foods. These foods are all-natural foods that have been part of our diet for millions of years.

The Paleo diet allows the following foods:

- **Certain vegetable oils like coconut oil, virgin olive oil and avocado oil.**
- **Eggs.**
- **Fruits.**
- **Meats.**
- **Nuts.**
- **Seafood.**
- **Vegetables.**

The Paleo diet isn't an easy diet to stick to in this day and age. Strict Paleo dieters have to really watch what they eat, since much of the food sold in stores is processed or has chemicals additives in it.

Finding raw, healthy food isn't as easy as it should be and Paleo dieters have to really pay attention to what they're putting in their bodies. One good way to avoid many non-Paleo foods is to avoid shopping in the aisles in the grocery store and to stick to the perimeter. You'll still find some processed food on the perimeter, but that's the area where most of the Paleo foods will be found. Fruits, vegetables and meats are almost always found on the perimeter of grocery stores.

Processed foods and foods with synthetic additives aren't allowed. The following foods are eliminated from the Paleo diet:

- **Anything with processed or refined sugars.**
- **Foods made with cereal grains or grain byproducts containing gluten.**
- **Foods with synthetic or processed ingredients.**
- **Highly refined or processed cooking oils.**
- **Legumes.**
- **Processed foods.**
- **Processed meats.**

Wheat flour is made from grain, so any bread made with wheat flour has to be eliminated. That eliminates most of the bread on store shelves.

Breads are one of the most difficult items to give up because they're so ingrained into the Western diet they're often consumed at every meal. We eat toast, bagels, muffins and pancakes for breakfast. For lunch, we have sandwiches made with bread and dinner sees us eating dinner rolls, buns and all sorts of baked goods. There's even more bread for dessert in the form of pastries, cupcakes, cakes, etc. Most people don't think about how much bread they're eating until they try to give it up.

There is some gray area in the Paleo diet. Spend any amount of time researching Paleo eating and you'll find countless questions from people about whether or not a specific food is Paleo.

One such gray area is milk and milk products. Strict Paleo dieters completely eliminate milk and milk products from their diet, while others make exceptions for probiotic milk products like yogurt and kefir. There are also some Paleo dieters who make exceptions for pastured butter in order to allow more flexibility in their baked goods. I've tried to keep milk products in the recipes in this book to a minimum in order to include strict Paleo dieters.

This book is tailored to the Paleo diet, but don't let that scare you away if you aren't a Paleo dieter. It contains good information for anybody on a gluten-free diet. You don't have to be Paleo to enjoy the many recipes contained herein.

What is Gluten?

From a scientific standpoint, gluten is a naturally occurring combination of proteins found in the endosperm of grass grains like wheat, barley and rye. It's used by developing plant embryos as a source of energy during germination.

Gluten is used in food for the following reasons:

- **As a leavening agent that helps food rise and keep its shape as it rises.**
- **To enhance or improve the texture of the food.**
- **To enhance the flavor.**
- **To thicken the food, as is the case with soups, broths, gravies and many condiments.**

When wheat is ground into flour and the flour is made into dough, the gluten in the flour adds texture and elasticity to the final product. Kneading dough links gluten molecules together, causing the protein molecules to bind to one another. Think of gluten as being the "glue" that bonds bread dough molecules together and you'll start to get the picture. The more dough with gluten in it is kneaded, the chewier the final product becomes.

When added to baked goods containing yeast, gluten traps carbon dioxide released by the yeast when it's heated, causing the dough to rise while keeping it together. There are ways to get bread to rise without gluten, but it's the easiest and most controllable method, which is a big reason why it's included in most bread recipes. Breads made without gluten tend to be denser and chewier than those made with flour containing gluten.

Is Gluten Bad?

Gluten in and of itself isn't necessarily bad, but a large percentage of the population has at least some level of sensitivity to it. Just how many people are actually sensitive to gluten isn't known because those who are sensitive to gluten suffer a wide array of symptoms and there is no standardized test capable of identifying all levels of sensitivity. Some people can go their whole lives suffering the symptoms of gluten sensitivity without realizing the source of their health issues.

What is known is there are multiple levels of gluten sensitivity. Some people are highly allergic to gluten, while others are only mildly irritated by it.

Gluten Intolerance

Gluten intolerance can be characterized by symptoms ranging from severe to mild. Gluten intolerance evokes an immune system response that is highly individual.

Some people are only mildly intolerant, suffering minor symptoms they may never relate to consumption of gluten. These people often go undiagnosed. There is no reliable test to check for this type of sensitivity, so the only way to find out whether or not you're sensitive to gluten is to cut it out of your diet and see if the symptoms you're having subside.

Others are highly intolerant of gluten and can suffer severe side effects. The immune system response in these individuals is much stronger than it is in those who are only mildly intolerant, but falls short of the intestinal damage suffered by those with celiac disease. People suffering high levels of gluten intolerance can experience moderate to severe joint pain, stomachaches, gas, diarrhea and a number of other symptoms related to this intolerance.

Celiac Disease

The most sensitive individuals are those with celiac disease, which is a digestive disorder in which gluten does actual damage to the small intestine every time a food containing gluten is consumed. In the worst cases, portions of the small intestines have to be removed because of extensive irreversible damage.

Celiac disease is characterized by sharp pains in the abdomen, severe side effects and the failure of the body to absorb nutrients from food. Approximately 1% of the population, or 1 in 100 people, have celiac disease. It's estimated that there are 2.5 million people in America alone who suffer celiac disease and are undiagnosed. The longer these people go without getting diagnosed, the more at risk they are of doing permanent damage to their digestive system.

Here are some of the symptoms associated with celiac disease:

- **Abdominal swelling.**
- **Bloating.**
- **Constipation.**
- **Depression.**
- **Diarrhea or loose stools.**
- **Failure to absorb nutrients from food.**
- **Fatigue.**
- **Gas.**
- **Inability to focus.**
- **Irritability.**
- **Lack of energy.**

- **Lethargy.**
- **Memory problems.**
- **Respiratory problems.**
- **Stomach distress or pain.**
- **Vomiting.**
- **Weight loss, even when you're eating good.**

Celiac disease can manifest itself in symptoms you wouldn't normally relate with a digestive disorder. It weakens the immune system, so sufferers of celiac disease can suffer a number of illnesses or ailments affecting other areas of the body.

There are autoantibodies in the blood of some celiac disease sufferers that can be identified through blood testing. While the presence of these autoantibodies usually indicates a patient has celiac disease, the lack thereof doesn't prove a person doesn't have the disease. Doctors seeking to rule out or confirm a celiac disease diagnosis may opt to perform an intestinal biopsy to check for the tell-tale damage to the small intestine.

Once diagnosed, the only "treatment" for celiac disease is eliminating gluten from the diet. Sufferers of celiac disease have to avoid gluten for the rest of their lives or risk doing permanent damage to their small intestines. Ingesting even small amounts of gluten can touch off a serious immune system response that has long-term consequences.

Here are just some of the long-term health conditions associated with gluten consumption by those who have celiac disease:

- **Anemia.**

- **Autoimmune disorders.**
- **Infertility.**
- **Mineral deficiencies.**
- **Nervous system disorders.**
- **Neurological disorders.**
- **Osteoporosis.**
- **Some cancers.**
- **Vitamin deficiencies.**

As you can see, the stakes are extremely high. Patients diagnosed early in life are able to manage the disease and are less likely to develop severe health conditions. If you suspect you're suffering from celiac disease, discuss your options with your physician.

Identifying Foods that Have Gluten

Gluten is added to a wide variety of foods to enhance their flavor and protein content and to help bind them together. While it's easy to identify the obvious foods that contain gluten like breads, pastas and breakfast cereal, gluten pops up in a number of unexpected places. It's used as a thickening agent in gravies, soups and broths and is found in some dairy products and liquors.

Any food made with the following ingredients will have gluten in it:

- **Barley malt.**
- **Barley.**
- **Bleached flour.**
- **Bread flour.**
- **Brewer's yeast.**
- **Brown flour.**
- **Bulgur.**
- **Cereal binding.**
- **Couscous.**
- **Durum wheat.**
- **Enriched flour.**
- **Farina.**
- **Graham flour.**
- **Hordeum vulgare.**
- **Kamut.**
- **Malt extract.**
- **Malt flavoring.**
- **Malt vinegar.**

- **Malt.**
- **Rye.**
- **Secale cereale.**
- **Seitan.**
- **Spelt.**
- **Triticale.**
- **Triticum spelta.**
- **Triticum vulgare.**
- **Wheat bran.**
- **Wheat flour.**
- **Wheat germ.**
- **Wheat protein.**
- **Wheat starch.**
- **Wheat.**
- **White flour.**
- **Whole wheat flour.**

Keep in mind this is only a partial list and manufacturers are constantly adding new ingredients that contain gluten to their products. They aren't required to disclose whether or not a product contains gluten and they know some people won't buy products with gluten in them, so don't expect products to say "gluten" on the label.

In addition to the above ingredients, which always indicate a food contains gluten, the presence of the following ingredients may also indicate gluten is present in a product:

- **Baking powder.**
- **Clarifying agents.**
- **Dextrin.**

- Emulsifiers.
- Enzymes.
- Flavorings.
- Ground spices.
- Hydrolyzed proteins.
- Maltodextrin.
- Miso.
- Modified food starch.
- Modified starch.
- Natural and artificial flavors.
- Seasonings.
- Stabilizers.
- Starch.
- Tocopherols.
- Vegetable protein.
- Vegetable starch.

To be clear, these ingredients don't always indicate the presence of gluten, but they are sometimes made using gluten-containing grains. When in doubt, contact the manufacturer and ask.

Grains containing gluten can be processed into a vast array of ingredients used in processed foods. Because of this, gluten pops up in a number of places you may not expect to find gluten. Here's a partial list of the many foods in which you might find gluten:

- Beer.
- Breads and baked goods.
- Cake.
- Candy, especially chocolate.

- Cereal.
- Certain types of alcohol.
- Coffees and teas.
- Condiments.
- Cookie dough.
- Cookies.
- Dry roasted nuts.
- Flavored beverages.
- Imitation meats and seafood.
- Medication.
- Non-dairy creamer.
- Pasta.
- Rice.
- Salad dressing.
- Sauces and gravies.
- Sausages and other processed meats.
- Soups, stews and broths.
- Soy sauce.
- Stuffing.
- Vitamins.

The easiest way to determine whether a food is gluten-free or not is to look for the words "gluten-free" on the label. Manufacturers know gluten-free foods are popular and will usually label their foods as being gluten-free when they don't contain any gluten. Don't assume a food is good for you just because it's labeled as being free of gluten. Manufacturers looking to make sales by placing the words "gluten-free" on the label may replace the gluten with additives and ingredients that are every bit as bad, if not worse, than gluten.

Additionally, there is the concern of cross-contamination, which occurs when foods that don't contain gluten are contaminated with gluten by foods that do contain it. This can happen during the manufacturing process, in the store or even at home, when foods are stored in close proximity. These are the toughest foods to identify because there won't be any gluten-containing ingredients on the label.

Gluten and the Paleo Diet

Paleo dieters avoid gluten because it isn't anything like the proteins our ancestors consumed. The glutens that are prevalent in the Western diet are processed to the point the body doesn't recognize them and we're eating significantly more gluten now than we ever have before.

Wheat and other cereal grains are a relative newcomer to the diet of humans and have only been a major staple for the last 10,000 or so years. While that may seem a long time when taken at face value, it's really only a drop in the evolutionary bucket when compared to the millions of years humans are believed to have been roaming the Earth. What this means is we've added large amounts of a food to our diet that our body isn't designed to eat.

The human body may eventually adapt to cereal grains and the gluten they contain, but it won't happen anytime soon. We may be seeing the signs of some people adapting, as certain people appear to be much more tolerant than others. If you are one of the folks lucky enough to be able to tolerate gluten, you can probably consume it in moderation without consequence.

The rest of us are better off avoiding it.

The Paleo diet is gluten-free by nature, since Paleo dieters don't consume grains containing gluten or processed foods, which are a major source of dietary gluten. Manufacturers are constantly finding new ways to sneak gluten into their products, so don't expect to be able to look at the ingredient listing and find "gluten" listed as one of the ingredients. Ah, if it were only so easy.

Be aware that while going Paleo means you've gone gluten-free as long as you stay disciplined, going gluten-free doesn't necessarily mean you've gone Paleo. There are a number of foods that are labeled "gluten-free" that don't conform to the Paleo diet.

It's up to the individual dieter to determine which foods are appropriate for their diet.

Homemade Ingredients

Some of the recipes in this book call for natural ingredients that can get a little pricey when you purchase them already made from the store. A number of these ingredients can easily be made at home, saving a significant amount of money in the process.

The recipes in this chapter set the foundation for many of the bread recipes found later in the book. You don't have to make them yourself, but I've found the homemade versions of these recipes taste better and they're generally less expensive than the commercial versions.

You get the added bonus of having control over everything that goes into the recipe, which allows you to ensure there are no harmful additives or cross-contaminated ingredients. That's an even bigger selling point for me than the price. There's something to be said about making your own Paleo breads entirely from raw ingredients. It's fulfilling and you know exactly what you're putting into your body when you eat it.

Almond Milk and Almond Flour

If you're buying almond milk from the grocery store and think you're eating healthy, you should check the label closely. The ingredients list should just say filtered water and almonds, because those are the only two items required to make almond milk. Instead, you'll see all sorts of additives that are there to increase shelf life and give the almond milk a uniform flavor.

Synthetic vitamins, carrageenan and all sorts of other unnecessary additives that aren't good for you can be found in commercial almond milk. These compounds are unnecessary and can negatively impact your health.

Almond flour isn't as bad, as you can find commercial products that use just almonds. The main concern with almond flour is the cost, as it is rather tough on the pocketbook. If you buy your almonds in bulk and make both almond milk and almond flour at the same time, you'll end up saving a decent amount of money in the end.

Yield: 10 cups almond milk and ½ cup almond flour

Pan Size: Baking tray.

Prep Time: 15 to 17 hours

Cook Time: 45 minutes

Ingredients:

2 cups raw almonds.

12 cups water.

1 teaspoon sea salt.

Directions:

1. Place the almonds into a bowl and add 2 cups of water to the bowl.
2. Add the sea salt and stir it in.
3. Leave the bowl to soak overnight. The almonds need to soak for at least 12 hours.
4. Discard the water in the bowl and rinse the almonds off with fresh water.
5. Transfer the almonds into a blender and add 10 cups of new water. If your blender can't hold that much, divide the almonds in half and do 2 batches with 5 cups of water at a time.
6. Blend until smooth. The almonds should be chopped into tiny pieces.
7. Pour the almond mixture into a nut bag and squeeze the liquid out of the almonds, collecting it in a bowl. Squeezing as much liquid as you can from the contents of the bag will speed up the drying time later on when you turn the almond meal into flour.
8. The liquid in the bowl is almond milk. Transfer it to an airtight glass container and store it in the fridge.
9. The contents of the bag can now be used to make almond flour. Line a baking tray with parchment paper.
10. Spread the almond meal out evenly across the baking tray.
11. Preheat the oven to its lowest setting.
12. Place the tray in the oven and heat the almond meal until it's free of moisture. This can take 3 to 4 hours

depending on how much moisture was left in the meal. Be careful not to over-dry or cook the almond meal.
13. Once the almond meal is dry, remove it from the oven and let it cool.
14. Place the meal into a blender and blend it on high until it's the texture you desire. Blending almond meal for too long will cause it to thicken up and become almond butter.

Storage:

Almond milk should be stored in the fridge and will last about a week. Almond flour will last months when stored in an airtight container in the fridge and can last up to a year when stored in the freezer.

Almond Butter

Almond butter is simple to make, but it takes a while. You're going to need a food processor with an S-blade and a lot of patience. It can also be made in the blender, but it's going to take even longer because you're going to have to frequently stop the blender to scrape the almonds off of the sides of the canister.

Yield: ¾ to 1 cup **Prep Time:** 20 minutes
Pan Size: None **Cook Time:** None

Ingredients:

3 to 4 cups raw almonds.

Directions:

1. Place the raw almonds in a food processor (or blender) with an S-shaped blade and process them on high until they turn into almond butter. This can take up to 20 minutes, so be patient.
2. Stop every minute or two and scrape the almonds off the sides of the canister. The almond butter is done when it's smooth and creamy.

Storage:

Almond butter can be kept at room temperature for a day or two, but should be stored in an airtight container in the refrigerator for longer-term storage because the oils in the butter will go rancid at room temperature. It will last up to 3 months in the fridge. If it starts to separate, stir the oils back into the solids. Don't eat almond butter that smells or tastes rancid.

Almond Meal

Almond meal and almond flour are often used interchangeably in recipes. Almond meal is similar to almond flour, in that it's made of finely ground almonds. The difference is almond meal is left grainier and isn't ground into as fine a powder as almond flour is. Almond meal is usually used in recipes where a grainier texture is desired.

Almond meal is simple to make, but you have to be careful not to blend it too much or it'll become almond flour or even almond butter. You want to chop the almonds you're processing into fine pieces, but stop short of them becoming powder and starting to release their natural oils.

It's difficult to grind almonds into pieces of uniform size. One trick you can use is to grind the almonds and then sift them to trap bigger pieces in the sifter. Pass the bigger pieces back through the blender or food processor and repeat the process until all of the almonds have been ground up.

Yield: 2 cups almond meal

Pan Size: Baking tray

Prep Time: 12 hours, 30 minutes

Cook Time: 45 minutes

Ingredients:

4 cups raw almonds.

Water.

Directions:

1. Place a pot on the stove and fill it with water. Bring the water to a boil.
2. Place the almonds into the pot and boil them for 2 minutes.
3. Drain the water away from the almonds and place them in a cool water bath to stop them from continuing to cook.
4. Squeeze the almonds at the larger end to pop them out of their skin. The skins should come right off.
5. Preheat the oven to 350° F.
6. Spread the almonds out on a baking tray and place the baking tray in the oven.
7. Dry the almonds for 15 minutes.
8. Set the tray out to dry for an additional 12 hours.
9. Process the almonds in a blender or food processor. Pulse the almonds until they're ground into small pieces. If you over-process them, they'll thicken into a paste and become almond butter.

Storage:

Almond meal should be stored in an airtight container in the fridge or the freezer. It can last a few months when properly stored.

Cashew Butter

Cashew butter is made the exact same way you make almond butter.

Add raw cashews to a blender or food processor and blend them until they become butter. You'll have to stop every minute or two and scrape the cashews off the sides. The cashews will break down and become butter much faster than almonds do because they contain more natural oil.

Coconut Milk and Coconut Flour

Here's another recipe that allows you to kill two birds with one stone. Like almond milk and almond flour, coconut milk and coconut flour are made at the same time. Also like almond milk, commercial coconut milk is often filled with unnecessary additives.

When you make coconut flour, the liquid you're left with is coconut milk. While coconut milk is relatively inexpensive to buy, coconut flour costs as much as $15 to $20 a pound when you buy the good stuff. You can save a significant amount of money making your own coconut flour and you'll end up with coconut milk in the process.

The amount of water you add to this recipe can be adjusted to change the consistency of the coconut milk. Add less water for thicker, creamier coconut milk and more water for thinner milk.

Yield: 7 to 8 cups milk and ~ 1 cup flour

Prep Time: 4 hours, 20 minutes

Pan Size: Baking tray

Cook Time: 45 minutes

Ingredients:

5 cups shredded unsweetened coconut.

8 cups water.

Directions:

1. Place the shredded coconut and water into a large bowl and stir it together.
2. Cover the bowl and let it sit at room temperature for 2 to 3 hours.
3. Place the contents of the bowl in a blender and blend on high until smooth.
4. Pour the contents of the blender into a nut milk bag.
5. Set a large bowl beneath the nut bag and squeeze as much liquid as you can out of the coconut and catch it in the bowl. The goal is to squeeze every last drop of liquid you can get out of the coconut before moving on to making coconut flour. The liquid in the bowl is coconut milk. Store it in an airtight container in the fridge.
6. The pulp that's left in the nut bag can now be processed into coconut flour.
7. Preheat your oven to 150° F. If your oven can't get this low, set it to the lowest setting.
8. Place the coconut pulp onto a baking tray and spread it out in a thin layer across the sheet.
9. Place the baking tray in the oven and let it cook until there isn't any moisture left in the coconut. This usually takes 45 minutes to an hour, but can vary depending on how much moisture is left in the coconut. Don't use too much heat and don't leave the coconut in the oven for too long or you'll end up with toasted coconut pulp instead of dried coconut that can be turned into flour.
10. Place the dried pulp into a food processor and blend it on high until it's ground into a fine powder.

Storage:

Coconut milk should be stored in the fridge and will last up to a week when properly stored. Coconut flour should be stored in an airtight container in the fridge and can last up to 6 months. Allow coconut flour to return to room temperature before using it in the recipes in this book.

Coconut Cream

Coconut cream is easy to make. You can make it with canned full-fat coconut milk or with coconut milk made using the previous recipe. If you plan on making coconut cream out of coconut milk you're making yourself, it's easier to do if you use less water when making the coconut milk so it's thicker to begin with. You're going to be separating the fat from the water, so the less water you start with, the better off you'll be.

In order to make coconut cream, take full-fat coconut milk and put in in the fridge. If you're using canned coconut milk, you can toss the can in the fridge. If you're using homemade coconut milk, put it in a glass container with a wide brim. After about 8 hours or so, the coconut cream will have separates from the milk and risen to the top.

Being in the fridge causes the fats to solidify, so you should be able to spoon the cream out of the container without too much trouble. You now have coconut cream that can be used in your recipes. Don't toss out the leftover liquid. This coconut water can be consumed as-is or used as a base for smoothies.

Coconut Oil

Coconut oil is one of my favorite vegetable oils. It's packed full of healthy fats and I've switched to using it for a number of cooking and baking tasks. I'm always on the lookout for new ways to incorporate this oil into my recipes.

Store-bought coconut oil is often heated during both the oil extraction and the pasteurization process, which kills the enzymes in the oil and renders it less beneficial than cold-pressed oils made at home. There are oils that are cold-pressed available in stores, so if you're buying the oil, seek out those oils.

The process of making coconut oil isn't as easy as the other ingredients in this section, but I'm including it just in case you want to make your own. There are pretty good deals on coconut oil online these days, so I rarely make it, but it's good to know how.

Yield: Varies.

Prep Time: 8 hours, 45 minutes

Pan Size: Baking tray

Cook Time: 45 minutes

Ingredients:

6 coconuts.

Directions:

1. Gather the coconuts. You want to use coconuts that have already turned brown on the outside.
2. Crack the coconut open using a meat cleaver.
3. Remove the meat from the coconut and wash the meat.
4. Chop the coconut into pieces with a food processor or blender. Be forewarned this step is going to take a tough blender. The coconut can be grated by hand first to make it easier to blend.
5. Blend the coconut until it's chopped into fine pieces. If you're having trouble blending the coconut, add a few tablespoons of water.
6. Place the ground coconut one cup at a time into a large piece of cheesecloth and hold it over a bowl. Create a bag out of the cheesecloth with the coconut in the middle. Squeeze as much liquid as you can get out of the coconut and into the bowl.
7. Repeat step 6 until you've processed all of the coconut. Save the pulp because you can use it to make coconut flour.
8. Pour the contents of the bowl into a glass container and move it to the fridge. It will separate into coconut milk and cream after about 8 hours.
9. Skim the cream off the top of the milk. You only want the thick cream at the top.
10. Place the cream into a pot and bring it to a simmer. The coconut remnants in the cream will solidify and start to turn brown and the liquid you're left with in the pot is coconut oil. It will take 30 to 45 minutes for this separation to occur.

Storage:

Coconut oil can be stored in an airtight container at room temperature for months. It can also be refrigerated, but will turn into a solid that has to be melted for most baking recipes.

Citrus Zest

Citrus zest is added to recipes to impart a slight citrus flavor to them. It's made from the peels of citrus fruit like lemons, oranges and limes. The peels contain the essential oils of the fruit, which are the compounds you smell when you bend the peel back and forth. They're the aromatic essence of the fruit and are thought to have a number of health benefits.

To zest a piece of fruit, you need to remove the peel from the fruit. This can be done using a special tool called a zester or you can use the small holes on a grater to grate the peel off of the fruit. Regardless of the method used, be careful not to remove any of the white pith. It has a strong bitter taste that will ruin the flavor of baked goods.

One medium-sized piece of fruit usually yields between one and two tablespoons of zest.

Sweet Paleo Breads

Most people think they have to give up sweet bread when they go on a gluten-free or Paleo diet. That couldn't be further from the truth, as there are a number of sweetened breads that can be made that don't contain gluten or non-Paleo ingredients.

This chapter covers breads that have a sweet taste to them. They use natural sugars like raw honey and maple syrup to sweeten the bread instead of the refined sugars found in traditional sweet bread recipes. They do contain some sugar, but it's natural sugar that's much better for you than the processed stuff found in most sweet bread recipes.

Keep in mind while eating these breads that they do still have sugar and consume them in moderation. They're better for you than regular breads that use processed sugars and refined wheat flour, but you still don't want to eat them in large amounts.

Almond Butter Bread

Prior to going gluten-free, I used to eat a lot of sandwiches. I'd sometimes have some form of sandwich for breakfast, lunch and dinner. I didn't give much thought to how much bread I was eating until after I went gluten-free. It was a difficult to stick with my decision because I thought I had to give up my beloved sandwiches.

Had I known about this recipe then, making the switch would have been a lot easier. Almond butter bread is great for sandwiches. Eggs, turkey, tri-tip. You name it. Pretty much any kind of meat goes well with this bread. It also works well for peanut butter and jelly sandwiches and I can make a mean toasted cheese sandwich with it as well.

Yield: 1 loaf

Pan Size: 8 ½ x 4 ½ bread pan

Prep Time: 10 minutes

Cook Time: 35 to 45 minutes

Ingredients:

6 eggs.

¾ cup coconut flour.

½ cup honey.

½ cup extra virgin coconut oil.

½ teaspoon sea salt.

Directions:

1. Combine the eggs, honey and coconut oil in a bowl.
2. Combine the coconut flour and sea salt in a separate bowl.
3. Combine the contents of the two bowls and mix them until blended.
4. Preheat the oven to 350° F.
5. Line an 8 ½ x 4 ½ bread pan with parchment paper.
6. Place the batter into the bread pan and work it down until it's settled into the bottom of the pan. The batter is going to be thick and difficult to work with.
7. Bake the bread for 35 to 45 minutes or until the edges are golden brown.
8. Let the bread cool for 10 minutes while in the pan. Remove the bread from the pan and let it cool for an additional 30 to 60 minutes.
9. Serve with honey, nut butter or jam.

Storage:

This bread must be consumed within a couple days if stored at room temperature. It'll last up to 5 days in the fridge and a month or more when stored in the freezer.

Apple Cinnamon Nut Bread

We've all heard the saying, "An apple a day keeps the doctor away." I don't know if that hold true for this nut bread, but I wouldn't mind eating a slice of it every day. It's really that good.

I've tried making this recipe with a variety of apples and have found Granny Smith apples taste the best. These tart, crisp apples don't go as soft during baking as some apple types do and the tartness balances nicely against the sweet bread. If you want sweeter bread, try sweeter red apple varieties. Bread made with sweeter apple types is a little too sweet for my tastes, but it'll fit the bill if you're craving something sweet.

Yield: 1 loaf

Pan Size: 9 x 5 bread pan

Prep Time: 10 minutes

Cook Time: 30 to 40 minutes

Bread Ingredients:

3 eggs.

2 apples.

1 ½ cups almond flour.

¼ cup extra virgin coconut oil.

3 tablespoons coconut flour.

3 tablespoons raw honey.

1 tablespoon cinnamon.

½ teaspoon baking soda.

½ teaspoon sea salt.

Topping Ingredients:

¼ cup chopped pecans.

2 tablespoons raw honey.

1 teaspoon cinnamon.

Directions:
1. Peel the apples and dice them.
2. Warm the coconut oil up gently until it melts and pour it into a bowl.
3. Beat the eggs and add them to the coconut oil.
4. Stir in the rest of the bread ingredients and mix together thoroughly.
5. Preheat the oven to 350° F.
6. Grease a 9 x 5 bread pan with coconut oil.
7. Place the batter into the bread pan and spread it out evenly.
8. Bake the bread for 30 to 40 minutes or until the edges are golden brown and a toothpick inserted into the center comes out clean.
9. Let the bread cool for 10 minutes while in the pan. Remove the bread from the pan and let it cool for an additional 30 to 60 minutes before serving.
10. Prepare the topping while the bread is cooling. Combine the topping ingredients in a bowl. Once

the bread is done cooling, sprinkle the coated pecans on top of the bread.

Storage:

This bread must be consumed within a couple days if stored at room temperature. It'll last up to 5 days in the fridge and a month or two when stored in an airtight container in the freezer.

Banana Bread

It seems I always have bananas that are turning spotty and are right on the verge of going bad. Once they reach that point, nobody wants to eat them and I hate for them to go to waste, so I use them to make this banana bread recipe. It's funny how overripe bananas no one wants can be added to a recipe and turned into something everyone wants. This banana bread rarely lasts more than a day or two on the counter.

Try adding dark chocolate chips to this recipe if the diet you're on allows for it.

Yield: 1 loaf.

Pan Size: 8 ½ x 4 ½ bread pan

Prep Time: 10 minutes

Cook Time: 40 to 50 minutes

Ingredients:

3 ripe bananas.

5 eggs.

5 dates.

½ cup coconut flour.

4 tablespoons almond butter.

2 tablespoons coconut oil.

2 teaspoons cinnamon.

1 teaspoon baking soda.

A pinch of salt.

Directions:

1. Remove the seeds from the dates and peel the bananas. Mash the bananas in a bowl and blend them with the dates.
2. Add the rest of the ingredients and blend them together until thoroughly mixed.
3. Preheat the oven to 350° F.
4. Line an 8 ½ x 4 ½ bread pan with parchment paper.
5. Fill the bread pan with batter.
6. Bake the bread for 40 to 50 minutes or until the edges are golden brown and a toothpick inserted in the center comes out clean.
7. Let the bread cool for 10 minutes while in the pan. Remove the bread from the pan and let it finish cooling on a wire rack.

Storage:

This bread will last a couple days on the counter. For longer-term storage, move the bread to the freezer and store it in an airtight container.

Blueberry Lemon Nut Bread

A variation of this recipe has been in my family for years. Of course it wasn't Paleo and had to be modified for this book, but I'm pleased with the way it turned out. It's almost indistinguishable from the original recipe, which is difficult to do when transforming regular baked goods into Paleo dishes.

This recipe can be modified to make a number of other breads.

You can eliminate the blueberries and you'll have lemon nut bread, which is pretty good on its own. Or you can eliminate the lemon and just make blueberry nut bread which is also pretty good. I prefer the combination of blueberries and lemon because the tartness of the lemon complements the sweetness of the blueberries. Add the flavor of the walnuts to the mix and you've got something special!

Yield: 1 loaf

Pan Size: 8 ½ x 4 ½ bread pan

Prep Time: 15 minutes

Cook Time: 40 to 50 minutes

Bread Ingredients:

2 cups almond flour.

1 cup fresh blueberries.

1 cup walnuts, chopped.

3 eggs.

½ cup coconut oil.

¼ cup coconut milk.

5 tablespoons raw honey.

2 tablespoons almond butter.

3 teaspoons lemon zest.

2 teaspoons pure vanilla extract.

1 teaspoon baking soda.

½ teaspoon sea salt.

Glaze Ingredients:

1 tablespoon honey.

1 tablespoon lemon juice.

Directions:

1. Gently heat the coconut oil in a saucepan until it melts. Add it to a bowl with the eggs, coconut milk, honey, almond butter, lemon zest and vanilla extract and whisk them all together.
2. Combine the almond flour, baking soda and sea salt in a separate bowl and blend them together.
3. Combine the contents of the two bowls and mix until barely incorporated.
4. Fold the blueberries and walnuts into the batter.
5. Preheat the oven to 350° F.
6. Line the bread pan with parchment paper.

7. Transfer the contents of the bowl to the bread pan and level the batter out.
8. Bake for 40 to 50 minutes or until the top of the bread is golden brown and the bread is cooked all the way through.
9. Let bread cool for 10 minutes in the pan and then transfer it to a wire rack to finish cooling.
10. While the bread is cooling, make the glaze by combining the lemon and honey and whisking them together.
11. Use a toothpick to poke a bunch of holes in the top of the loaf. This will allow the glaze to work its way down into the loaf.
12. Brush the glaze onto the top of the loaf and let it dry before serving.

Storage:

This bread must be consumed within a couple days if stored at room temperature. It'll last up to a week in the fridge and a month or two when stored in an airtight container in the freezer. It's best to store this bread without the glaze added. Make it and add it when you're ready to serve the bread.

Carrot Cake

Carrot cake is a comfort food for me. It brings back memories of summers spent at my grandma's house waiting for all sorts of baked goods to finish cooking. One of my favorites was her special carrot cake, fresh out of the oven. I used to try to convince my grandma it was good for me because it had carrots in it, so I could get an extra piece. It always worked, but now that I look back on it, I think she may have just been playing along.

Yield: 1 loaf

Pan Size: 8 x 8 baking dish

Prep Time: 15 minutes

Cook Time: 40 to 50 minutes

Ingredients:

3 eggs.

2 cups shredded carrots.

1 ½ cups coconut flour.

4 tablespoons honey.

4 tablespoons extra virgin coconut oil.

½ tablespoon cinnamon.

½ teaspoon nutmeg.

½ teaspoon baking soda.

½ teaspoon sea salt.

OPTIONAL: ½ cup raisins.

OPTIONAL: ½ cup chopped walnuts or pecans.

Directions:

1. Combine the coconut flour, cinnamon, nutmeg, baking soda and sea salt in a bowl.
2. Combine the eggs, honey and coconut oil in a separate bowl.
3. Fold the contents of the 1st bowl into the contents of the 2nd bowl until incorporated.
4. Fold the carrots into the batter. Add the nuts and raisins and fold them in now, if desired.
5. Preheat the oven to 350° F.
6. Grease a glass 8 x 8 baking dish with coconut oil and pour the batter into it.
7. Bake the carrot cake for 40 to 50 minutes or until a toothpick inserted into the center of the cake comes out clean.

Storage:

Paleo carrot cake can be stored in the fridge for up to a week or in the freezer for up to 3 months.

Cinnamon Bread

Make this bread for dessert when you have guests over and you'll have them practically begging for the recipe. The coconut cream cinnamon topping is optional, but once you try it, you aren't going to want to make this bread without it. For best results, top the bread with the topping right before you serve it or serve the bread with little cups of the topping to dip it in.

Yield: 1 loaf

Pan Size: 9 x 5 bread pan

Prep Time: 20 minutes

Cook Time: 30 to 40 minutes

Shortcake Ingredients:

3 eggs.

1 ripe banana.

1 ½ cups almond flour.

¼ cup coconut flour.

¼ cup raw honey.

¼ cup coconut oil.

1 ½ teaspoons cinnamon.

1 teaspoon vanilla extract.

½ teaspoon baking soda.

¼ teaspoon sea salt.

Whipped Topping Ingredients:

2 cans full-fat coconut milk.

2 tablespoons honey.

1 teaspoon vanilla extract.

1 tablespoon cinnamon.

Directions:

1. Combine the eggs, honey, vanilla and coconut oil in a bowl.
2. Add the almond flour, coconut flour, cinnamon, baking soda and sea salt to a separate bowl and mix them thoroughly.
3. Combine the contents of the two bowls and mix them together. Mash the banana and stir it in until incorporated.
4. Preheat the oven to 350° F.
5. Grease a 9 x 5 bread pan and fill it with the batter.
6. Cook the bread for 30 to 40 minutes or until the top is golden brown and a toothpick inserted into the center comes out clean.
7. Let the bread cool in the tin for 10 minutes. Transfer it to a wire cooling rack and let it cool for an additional 15 minutes before eating or prepping for storage.
8. To make the whipped frosting, place 2 cans of full-fat coconut milk in the fridge the day before you plan on making it. When you open the cans, there will be a layer of coconut cream at the top of the can. Scoop out the cream and add it to a bowl.

9. Blend it with a stick blender until it becomes light and frothy.
10. Add the honey, cinnamon and vanilla and whip them into the topping.
11. Cover the bread with the topping right before you serve it.

Storage:

This bread will last a few days on the counter, but should be stored in an airtight container in the fridge or freezer if you want to keep it for longer than that. It'll last up to a couple days in the fridge and a month or two in the freezer.

Cranberry Bread

My family has a traditional Thanksgiving dinner. Every year, we meet at a different family member's house and that member is responsible for all of the cooking. This year it was my turn and I made the decision to cook a Paleo Thanksgiving dinner. I was a bit nervous as to how it would turn out, but thanks to recipes like this one it was a huge success. Everything turned out so good I've been asked to help my brother, who's responsible for next year's dinner.

If the bread is too dry for your tastes, you can eliminate some of the coconut flour or you can add an extra egg or two. Don't attempt to cut this bread before it cools or you're going to have nothing but crumbs. It's best when left to sit overnight instead of eating it the day it's made.

Yield: 1 loaf

Pan Size: 9 x 5 bread pan

Prep Time: 15 minutes

Cook Time: 50 to 60 minutes

Ingredients:

6 eggs.

1 cup cranberries.

1 ripe banana.

¾ cup fresh orange juice.

¾ cup coconut flour.

¼ cup honey.

¼ cup extra virgin coconut oil.

1 ½ teaspoons baking powder.

1 teaspoon baking soda.

1 teaspoon orange zest.

1 teaspoon sea salt.

OPTIONAL: 1 cup chopped walnuts.

Directions:

1. Combine the coconut flour, baking powder, baking soda, orange zest and sea salt in a bowl.
2. Melt the coconut oil if it isn't already melted.
3. In a separate bowl, blend the eggs, banana, orange juice, honey and coconut oil.
4. Combine the contents of the two bowls and blend until smooth.
5. Gently crush the cranberries and fold them into the batter. If you're adding walnuts, add them now and fold them in.
6. Preheat the oven to 350° F.
7. Line the bread pan with parchment paper.
8. Pour the batter into the bread pan and level it out.
9. Bake for 50 to 60 minutes or until a toothpick inserted into the center comes out clean.
10. Let this bread completely cool before attempting to cut it or it will break apart. Cool the bread for ten minutes in the pan and transfer it to a wire rack to finish cooling.

Storage:

This bread will keep for a couple days at room temperature. Store it in an airtight container in the fridge for up to a week or move it to the freezer where it'll last for a couple months.

Fruitcake

My friends tell me I may be the only person on the planet who actually likes fruitcake. Well, it's true. I do like fruit cake and I'm not ashamed to admit it. Just in case there's anyone else out there like me, here's a Paleo version of fruitcake. If nothing else, you can make it and hand it out as gifts to annoy your friends who make fun of you for liking fruitcake.

Don't be afraid to substitute dried fruits into and out of this recipe. If there are dried fruit varieties you like that aren't in the recipe, you can probably add them to good effect. If you eliminate any of the fruit, substitute more of the other fruit types to make up for it.

Yield: 1 loaf

Pan Size: 9 x 5 bread pan

Prep Time: 10 minutes

Cook Time: 45 to 55 minutes

Ingredients:

5 eggs.

1 cup almond butter

½ cup tapioca flour.

¼ cup honey.

2 teaspoons apple cider vinegar.

1 teaspoon baking soda.

1 teaspoon cinnamon.

½ teaspoon sea salt.

A handful of dried blueberries.

¼ cup raisins.

¼ cup dried cranberries.

¼ cup dried apricots.

¼ cup dried mangoes.

Directions:

1. Add the eggs, almond butter, honey and apple cider vinegar to a bowl and blend it thoroughly with a stick blender. Alternatively, they can be blended in a stand mixer.
2. Combine the tapioca flour, baking soda, cinnamon and sea salt in a separate bowl and mix them together.
3. Fold the dry ingredients into the wet ingredients. Make sure they're incorporated, but don't over-mix them.
4. Fold the dried fruit into the batter.
5. Preheat the oven to 350° F.
6. Grease a bread pan with coconut oil and fill it with the batter.
7. Place the pan in the oven and bake it for 45 to 55 minutes. The bread is done when a toothpick inserted into the loaf comes out clean.
8. Let the bread cool for ten minutes in the pan. Remove it from the pan and let it finish cooling on a wire rack.

Storage:

This bread tastes best if left to sit for at least 12 hours. It'll last a few days at room temperature. It can be stored in the fridge for up to a week. It can be frozen and will last up to 6 months in the freezer.

Lemon Poppy Seed bread

Dessert time can't come soon enough when this bread's in the oven. It's lightly sweet and the texture is reminiscent of pound cake. It can be made with or without the lemon glaze, but I've found adding the glaze softens the bread up a bit and keeps it moist.

Be aware that eating foods with a lot of poppy seeds in them can cause you to fail certain drug tests, so if you're looking for a job or work somewhere you're tested regularly, it's probably a good idea to steer clear of this bread.

Yield: 1 loaf

Pan Size: 9 x 5 bread pan

Prep Time: 15 minutes

Cook Time: 35 to 45 minutes

Bread Ingredients:

7 eggs.

3 tablespoons coconut milk.

¾ cup coconut flour.

½ cup coconut oil.

½ cup raw honey.

5 tablespoons fresh lemon juice.

2 tablespoons lemon zest.

2 tablespoons poppy seeds.

1 teaspoon baking soda.

½ teaspoon sea salt.

Lemon Glaze Ingredients:

3 tablespoons coconut oil.

3 tablespoons raw honey.

3 tablespoons coconut milk.

1 tablespoon lemon zest.

2 tablespoons fresh lemon juice.

Directions:
1. Combine the eggs, coconut milk, coconut oil, honey and lemon juice in a bowl and mix them together.
2. Add the rest of the ingredients to the bowl and mix well.
3. Preheat the oven to 350° F.
4. Grease a 9 x 5 bread pan with coconut oil.
5. Pour the batter into the pan and make sure it's spread evenly.
6. Bake the bread for 35 to 45 minutes or until the top turns golden brown.
7. Remove the bread from the oven the let it cool.
8. While the bread is cooling, make the glaze.
9. Add all of the lemon glaze ingredients to a saucepot over low heat and bring it to a simmer, stirring constantly.
10. Remove the glaze from the heat and let it cool.

11. Once the glaze and the bread are both cool, poke a bunch of holes in the top of the loaf and pour the glaze over the top of the bread.
12. Move the bread to the fridge and let it sit for an hour or two while the glaze soaks into the bread.

Storage:

Store this bread in the fridge until you're ready to eat it. It'll last up to a week. If you want to keep it in the freezer, you can, but wait until you're ready to eat it to add the glaze.

Pecan Raisin Bread

The original version of this recipe called for cashews instead of pecans. I thought the cashews were too sweet and like the pecans better, but that may just be because I've never been a big fan of cashews. If you like cashews, try substituting equal amounts of chopped cashews for the pecans. You could also sub in walnuts if that's your preference.

Yield: 1 loaf

Pan Size: 9 x 5 bread pan

Prep Time: 10 minutes

Cook Time: 30 to 40 minutes

Ingredients:

4 eggs.

1 cup almond flour.

½ cup chopped pecans.

½ cup raisins.

4 tablespoons raw honey.

5 tablespoons coconut flour.

1 tablespoon cinnamon.

1 teaspoon vanilla.

½ teaspoon baking soda.

½ teaspoon nutmeg.

½ teaspoon sea salt.

Directions:

1. Combine all of the ingredients except the pecans and raisins in a bowl and blend them together.
2. Fold the pecans and raisins into the batter.
3. Preheat the oven to 350° F.
4. Grease the bread pan with coconut oil.
5. Pour the batter into the pan and make sure it's level.
6. Bake the bread for 30 to 40 minutes or until a toothpick inserted into the center of the bread comes out clean.
7. Let the bread cool in the pan for at least 15 minutes. Remove the bread from the pan and let it finish cooling on a wire rack.

Storage:

This bread is best when left to sit for at least 12 hours before cutting and serving it. It can be stored in an airtight container in the fridge for up to a week and will last a month or two in the freezer.

Strawberry Shortcake

The first time I made this shortcake, I topped it with strawberries. It was good, but it was missing something. Then it hit me. It needed whipped cream. It would have been easy to grab a container of whipped cream, but I decided to create Paleo version of whipped cream that can be eaten by even those on a strict Paleo diet.

Yield: 8 to 10 shortcakes
Pan Size: Baking sheet
Prep Time: 20 minutes
Cook Time: 15 to 20 minutes

Shortcake Ingredients:

3 eggs.

4 cups almond flour.

3 teaspoons raw honey.

2 tablespoons coconut oil.

2 tablespoons fresh lemon juice.

1 teaspoon vanilla extract.

1 teaspoon baking soda.

¼ teaspoon sea salt.

Whipped Topping Ingredients:

2 cups full-fat coconut milk.

2 cups strawberries, stemmed and sliced.

2 tablespoons honey.

1 teaspoon vanilla extract.

Directions:

1. Combine the eggs, honey, lemon juice, vanilla and coconut oil in a bowl.
2. Add the almond flour, baking soda and sea salt and stir it in.
3. Preheat the oven to 350° F.
4. Line 10 wells in a muffin tin with cupcake liners. Grease the liners lightly with coconut oil.
5. Divide the batter amongst the wells.
6. Place the muffin tin in the oven and cook for 15 to 20 minutes or until the shortcakes are golden brown on top and a toothpick inserted into the center comes out clean.
7. Let the shortcakes cool in the tin for 10 minutes. Transfer them to a wire cooling rack and let them cool for an additional 15 minutes before eating or prepping for storage.
8. To make the whipped frosting, place 2 cans of full-fat coconut milk in the fridge the day before you plan on making it. Open the cans. There will be a layer of coconut cream at the top of the can. Scoop out the cream.
9. Place the cream into a bowl and blend it with a stick blender until it becomes light and frothy.
10. Add the honey and vanilla and whip it into the topping.
11. Slice the strawberries and mix them into the topping.

12. Cover the shortcakes with topping right before you serve them.

Storage:

These shortcakes should be stored in an airtight container in the fridge or freezer. They'll last up a couple days in the fridge and a month or two in the freezer.

Sweet Potato Bread

When made right, sweet potato bread is sweet and perfectly moist. When it's done wrong, you end up with a damp, dense bread that's difficult to stomach. I've tried a lot of Paleo sweet potato bread recipes and finally settled on this one as a near-perfect example of what sweet potato bread is supposed to be.

Yield: 1 loaf

Pan Size: 8 ½ x 4 ½ bread pan

Prep Time: 10 minutes

Cook Time: 60 to 70 minutes

Ingredients:

6 eggs.

2 roasted sweet potatoes.

¾ cup coconut flour.

4 tablespoons coconut milk.

1 teaspoon baking soda.

1 tablespoon lemon juice.

¼ teaspoon sea salt.

Directions:

1. Remove the sweet potato flesh from the skin and place the flesh in a bowl.

2. Add the rest of the ingredients to the bowl and blend everything together with a stick blender.
3. Preheat the oven to 350° F.
4. Grease a bread pan and pour the batter into the pan. Spread it out evenly.
5. Bake the bread for 40 minutes. Cover it with foil and bake if for an additional 20 to 30 minutes or until a toothpick inserted in the center comes out clean.
6. Let the bread cool for 15 minutes. Remove it from the pan and let it finish cooling on a wire rack.

Storage:

Store sweet potato bread in the fridge for up to a week. It can be stored in the freezer in an airtight container for up to a month.

Zucchini Bread

This is going to seem strange to those of you who eat it regularly, but I'd never heard of zucchini bread until a few years ago. To be completely honest with you, I'd never even considered adding zucchini to my bread recipes. Then one day I came across a recipe for zucchini bread in one of my books and was in the mood for something new. Little did I know I was about to discover a new favorite type of bread. There's something about the way the flavor of the zucchini melds with lightly sweetened bread that I can't resist.

There are a ton of zucchini bread recipes out there for non-Paleo eater. There aren't very many recipes for Paleo dieters, so I played around with an old recipe and came up with this zucchini bread. The key to getting this recipe just right is to use both almond flour and some coarser almond meal. The flour needs to be ground up as fine as you can get it. The almond meal can be made using the recipe in the Homemade Ingredients chapter of the book.

Yield: 1 loaf

Pan Size: 9 x 5 bread pan

Prep Time: 20 minutes

Cook Time: 30 to 40 minutes

Ingredients:

3 eggs.

1 ripe banana.

1 ½ cups grated zucchini.

1 cup fine almond flour.

1 cup finely chopped walnuts.

½ cup coarse almond meal.

5 tablespoons raw honey.

2 tablespoons coconut oil.

1 teaspoon cinnamon.

1 teaspoon pure vanilla extract.

1 ½ teaspoons baking soda.

½ teaspoon sea salt.

Directions:

1. Combine the almond flour, walnuts, almond meal, cinnamon, baking soda and sea salt in a bowl.
2. Combine the rest of the ingredients (except for the zucchini) in a separate bowl. It helps if you mash the banana before adding it to the bowl.
3. Place the contents of both bowls in a stand mixer and blend them together thoroughly. You can do this step by hand, but it's going to take a bit of work.
4. Fold the zucchini into the batter.
5. Preheat the oven to 350° F.
6. Line the bread pan with parchment paper.
7. Pour the batter into the pan.
8. Place the pan in the oven and bake the bread for 30 to 40 minutes or until a toothpick inserted into the center of the loaf comes out clean.

9. Remove the pan from the oven and let it cool for 10 minutes.
10. Remove the bread from the pan and place it on a wire rack to finish cooling.

Storage:

Zucchini bread should be stored in the fridge. It'll last up to a week. It can be stored in an airtight container in the freezer, but tends to get really crumbly when thawed.

Traditional-Style Paleo Breads

In this section you'll find Paleo bread recipes designed to replace traditional bread recipes that normally use flour to make the dough or batter. Again, these recipes use all-natural ingredients that go through minimal processing to reach the state they're in when added to the recipe.

You'll find pizza dough, sandwich bread, bagels, hamburger buns and all sorts of other recipes that mimic traditional breads in this chapter. Some of the recipes are close facsimiles to the traditional breads, while others go above and beyond the breads you're used to both in flavor and health value.

Contrary to what some folks believe, going gluten-free doesn't mean eating bland, tasteless foods and these breads prove it.

Almond Meal Pancakes

These pancakes are more filling than traditional pancakes, so a single medium-sized pancake is usually enough to fill you up. Top them with fruit or real maple syrup and you've got breakfast covered for the whole family.

Yield: 4 to 8 pancakes
Pan Size: Skillet
Prep Time: 10 minutes
Cook Time: 5 to 10 minutes

Ingredients:

4 eggs.

2 cups shredded coconut.

2 cups coconut milk.

1 cup almond meal.

3 tablespoons almond butter.

1 teaspoon baking powder.

1 teaspoon sea salt.

½ teaspoon pure vanilla extract.

Directions:

1. Combine all of the ingredients and mix them together until completely blended.
2. Grease a skillet with coconut oil and heat it up over Medium heat.

3. Spoon the batter onto the skillet and press it down flat.
4. Cook until browned on one side and then flip the pancake over and cook it until brown on the other side.
5. Let cool for a couple minutes, add topping and serve.

Storage:

These pancakes are best if consumed right after they're cooked. They can be stored in the freezer and reheated in a toaster or toaster oven.

Simple Paleo Bagels

Here's a quick and easy Paleo bagel recipe. It calls for butter, but you can sub coconut oil in if you're avoiding milk products. These bagels are good with butter or garlic spread and they're really good when cut in half, toasted and used to make breakfast sandwiches.

This recipe is for basic bagels and can be used as a jumping off point to create other types of bagels. Try adding blueberries, raisins, poppy seeds, sesame seeds or any of your other favorite bagel ingredients.

Yield: 8 bagels

Pan Size: Baking tray

Prep Time: 20 minutes

Cook Time: 15 to 20 minutes

Ingredients:

2 eggs.

2 cups tapioca flour.

1 cup warm water.

½ cup coconut flour.

½ cup arrowroot powder.

½ cup butter (or coconut oil).

2 teaspoons baking powder.

1 teaspoon sea salt.

Directions:

1. Combine the wet ingredients and stir them together.
2. Add the rest of the ingredients minus the tapioca flour and stir them in.
3. Add the tapioca flour last and slowly mix it in to prevent clumping.
4. Let the dough sit for 10 minutes.
5. Roll the dough into balls and press your finger into the center to form round bagels with a hole in the center.
6. Preheat the oven to 350° F.
7. Place the bagels on a greased baking tray.
8. Brush the tops of the bagels with melted butter or coconut oil.
9. Bake them for 15 to 20 minutes or until they start to brown and feel crisp to the touch.
10. Let the bagels cool for 15 minutes before serving.

Storage:

Eat these bagels right away for best results. They can be stored for a day or two at room temperature. For longer-term storage, place them in an airtight container and move them to the freezer.

Cashew Butter Toast Bread

When I first went Paleo, I really struggled to find a bread recipe that can be used to make good toast. This recipe not only makes good toast, but it can be used for sandwiches as well. It's as close as you're probably going to get to real bread in a Paleo recipe.

Yield: 1 loaf.

Pan Size: 9 x 5 bread pan

Prep Time: 15 minutes

Cook Time: 30 to 40 minutes

Ingredients:

6 egg whites.

1 ½ cups cashew butter.

½ cup coconut flour.

½ cup coconut milk.

2 teaspoons apple cider vinegar.

1 teaspoon raw honey.

1 ½ teaspoons baking soda.

½ teaspoon sea salt.

Directions:

1. Preheat your oven to 350° F.
2. Beat the egg whites into the coconut milk. Add the raw honey and apple cider vinegar and beat them in.

3. Add the rest of the ingredients to the bowl and blend them with a stand mixer.
4. Line a bread pan with parchment paper.
5. Pour the batter into the bread pan and disperse it evenly.
6. Cook the bread for 30 to 40 minutes or until a toothpick inserted into the center comes out clean.
7. Let the bread cool in the pan for 10 minutes before removing it from the pan and letting it finish cooling on a wire rack.

Storage:

This bread is best after being stored in the fridge for a day or two. It can be stored in an airtight container in the freezer, but may get a bit dry.

Chestnut Bread

Are you looking for hearty bread with a slightly nutty flavor? This chestnut bread may fit the bill. This crust is thick and filling, while the interior is soft and light. It's good bread to serve as a side dish with meals. It also makes pretty good toast.

Yield: 1 loaf

Pan Size: 8 ½ x 4 ½ bread pan

Prep Time: 15 minutes

Cook Time: 20 to 30 minutes

Ingredients:

5 eggs.

3 cups chestnut flour.

2 cups almond meal.

2 tablespoons olive oil.

½ teaspoon sea salt.

1 ½ teaspoons baking soda.

Directions:

1. Combine the chestnut flour, almond meal, sea salt and baking soda in a bowl.
2. Whip the eggs. Add the olive oil and beat it into the eggs.
3. Combine the contents of the two bowls and knead them together.

4. Preheat the oven to 350° F.
5. Grease a bread pan and press the dough into the bread pan.
6. Brush the top of the loaf with olive oil or coconut oil.
7. Bake for 20 to 30 minutes or until the loaf is browned on top.
8. Let cool for 15 minutes in the bread pan and then transfer the loaf to a wire rack to finish cooling.

Storage:

This bread will last a couple days on the counter. It gets crumbly when stored in the fridge or freezer, so use it for toast once you move it to cold storage.

Coconut Bread

I'm not sure what exactly to make of this bread. It has a strong coconut flavor and tastes great, but is dense and a bit on the grainy side when it comes to texture. Don't get me wrong here . . . It's pretty good; I'm just having a tough time figuring out what to pair it with. For now, I'm just going to eat it as a snack whenever I want something filling and low on carbs.

Yield: 1 loaf

Pan Size: 8 ½ x 4 ½ bread pan

Prep Time: 10 minutes

Cook Time: 30 to 40 minutes

Ingredients:

8 eggs.

1 cup coconut flour.

¾ cup extra virgin coconut oil.

¾ cup shredded coconut.

½ teaspoons baking soda.

½ teaspoon sea salt.

1 teaspoon cinnamon.

Directions:

1. Combine the coconut flour, baking soda, sea salt and cinnamon in a bowl.

2. Add the eggs and coconut oil to the bowl and knead them in.
3. Fold in the shredded coconut.
4. Preheat the oven to 350° F.
5. Grease a bread pan with coconut oil and pour the batter into it.
6. Bake it for 30 to 40 minutes or until the edges start to brown and a toothpick inserted into the middle comes out clean.

Storage: This bread must be consumed within a couple days if stored at room temperature. It'll last up to 5 days in the fridge and few months when stored in an airtight container in the freezer.

Flaxseed Bread

For those not familiar with flaxseed, also known as linseed, it's a seed from the flax plant, which is a fiber crop that has origins in ancient Egypt. It's a healthy source of dietary fiber, micronutrients and beneficial fatty acids. Flaxseeds have to be either bought in ground form or they need to be ground before adding them to recipes, as whole flaxseeds will usually pass right through the digestive system.

This bread is light and spongy. If you want denser bread, try cutting back on the baking soda.

Yield: 1 loaf

Pan Size: 8 ½ x 4 ½ bread pan

Prep Time: 10 minutes

Cook Time: 30 to 40 minutes

Ingredients:

6 eggs.

1 ½ cups almond meal.

½ cup extra virgin coconut oil.

¼ cup ground flaxseed.

3 tablespoons coconut flour.

2 tablespoons apple cider vinegar.

1 ½ teaspoons baking soda.

¼ teaspoon sea salt.

Directions:

1. Combine the almond meal, ground flaxseed, coconut flour, baking soda and sea salt in a bowl.
2. Stir in the eggs, coconut oil and apple cider vinegar until completely combined.
3. Preheat the oven to 350° F.
4. Line the bread pan with parchment paper and pour the dough into the pan.
5. Bake the bread for 30 to 40 minutes or until a toothpick inserted in the center comes out clean.
6. Remove the bread from the oven and let it cool before serving.

Storage:

This bread must be consumed within a couple days if stored at room temperature. It'll last up to 5 days in the fridge and few months when stored in an airtight container in the freezer.

Garlic Herb Bread

Here's an herbed bread recipe that adds garlic, thyme, sage and parsley to the dough to give it an absolutely deliciously herby flavor. Sprinkle it with cheese to make cheesy herb bread or add a light coating of garlic spread to add even more garlic flavor. This bread goes great with most dinner dishes, but pairs best with Italian dishes.

No matter what you pair it with, I'll bet you can't eat just one slice.

Yield: 1 loaf

Pan Size: 8 ½ x 4 ½ bread pan

Prep Time: 10 minutes

Cook Time: 30 to 40 minutes

Ingredients:

6 eggs.

6 garlic cloves, peels and chopped into pieces.

2 cups almond flour.

½ cup extra virgin coconut oil.

½ cup ground flaxseed.

2 tablespoons coconut flour.

2 teaspoons baking soda.

1 teaspoon sea salt.

1 teaspoon thyme.

1 teaspoon sage.

1 teaspoon parsley.

Directions:

1. Combine the eggs and coconut oil in a bowl.
2. Add the rest of the ingredients minus the garlic to the bowl and blend them in.
3. Add the garlic to the bowl and fold it in.
4. Preheat the oven to 350° F.
5. Line an 8 ½ x 4 ½ bread pan with parchment paper.
6. Pour the batter into the bread pan.
7. Bake the bread for 30 to 40 minutes, or until the edges are golden brown.
8. Let the bread cool for 10 minutes while in the pan. Remove the bread from the pan and let it finish cooling on a wire rack.

Storage:

This bread must be consumed within a couple days if stored at room temperature. It'll last up to 5 days in the fridge and a month when stored in the freezer.

Hamburger Buns

Let me begin by saying these buns aren't like your average white flour hamburger buns. The spices give them a unique flavor that goes well with both hamburgers and turkey burgers. Once you try these buns, you'll never crave regular hamburger buns again.

Yield: 8 buns

Pan Size: Baking sheet

Prep Time: 20 minutes

Cook Time: 30 to 40 minutes

Ingredients:

3 eggs.

2 cloves of garlic.

1 cup tapioca flour.

½ cup arrowroot powder.

½ cup coconut flour.

1 cup water.

½ cup extra virgin olive oil.

2 teaspoons sea salt.

2 teaspoons sesame seeds.

Directions:

1. Warm up the water and stir the sea salt and olive oil into it.
2. Mince the garlic and add it to the bowl.
3. Stir in all of the ingredients except the tapioca flour. Add the tapioca flour last, stirring in a little bit at a time. This prevents the tapioca flour from clumping up.
4. Knead the dough. Divide it into 8 buns of similar size.
5. Preheat the oven to 350° F.
6. Lightly oil a baking sheet and place the buns on the sheet.
7. Bake the buns for 30 to 40 minutes or until they're lightly browned on the top and bottom

Storage:

These buns should be stored in an airtight container in the fridge or freezer. They'll last up to a week in the fridge and a month or two in the freezer.

Microwave Quick Bread

Here's a single-serving bread recipe that can be whipped up in a hurry. This recipe is designed for those times when you want bread and you want it fast. It can be made in less than 5 minutes from start to finish.

This bread is great for sandwiches or you can add a bit of almond butter or homemade preserves to it to make a quick breakfast snack for those mornings when you're running late and don't have time to cook a full meal. It's also fun to make with the kids because it provides almost-instant gratification.

Yield: 1 loaf

Pan Size: 1 coffee mug

Prep Time: 3 minutes

Cook Time: 1 to 2 minutes

Ingredients:

1 egg.

2 tablespoons almond meal.

¼ teaspoon baking soda.

¼ teaspoon apple cider vinegar.

A pinch of sea salt.

Directions:

1. Beat the egg.

2. Combine all of the ingredients in the coffee mug and stir them together.
3. Microwave for 1 to 2 minutes, or until the bread is cooked all the way through.
4. Let the bread cool for 5 minutes. Dump it out of the mug and cut it in half.

Storage:

Consume this bread immediately. It doesn't store well.

Paleo Seed and Nut Loaf

First, a funny story about this nut loaf.

I purchased a new patio set this summer and spent a number of summer evenings dining and enjoying a glass of wine or two while hanging out on the patio. I made this nut loaf and brought it outside to serve with dinner, which was cooking on the barbecue. I realized I'd forgotten something in the house and went inside, setting the nut loaf on the table.

Imagine my surprise when I returned to find a congregation of pigeons and blackbirds on the table tearing into my nut loaf. They'd completely torn it apart trying to get at the bounty of seeds and nuts inside the loaf. I was pretty angry at the time and remember demanding my husband take up hunting squab, but now that I look back on it, it's pretty funny.

I'm not sure whether this recipe qualifies as bread or not, since it doesn't use any nut flour whatsoever. Instead, it combines seeds and nuts with eggs and vegetable oil to form a "loaf" that's dense and extremely filling. It's also very tasty, but be careful not to overindulge. Since it's packed with nuts and seeds, it's higher in fat than most of the breads in this book. Keep your slices small and enjoy it in moderation.

The variety of nuts and seeds used in this recipe don't really matter. You can add and remove seeds and nuts as you see fit.

Yield: 1 loaf.

Pan Size: 8 ½ x 4 ½ bread pan

Prep Time: 10 minutes

Cook Time: 40 minutes

Ingredients:

6 eggs.

½ cup extra virgin coconut oil.

2 tablespoons honey.

2 teaspoons salt.

½ cup sliced almonds.

¼ cup chopped walnuts.

¼ cup pecans, chopped.

¼ cup pistachios, chopped.

½ cup pumpkin seeds.

½ cup sunflower seeds.

3 tablespoons linseeds.

3 tablespoons ground flaxseeds.

¼ cup sesame seeds.

Water.

Directions:

1. Combine all of the ingredients in a bowl and stir together until completely mixed. If the mixture seems too thick, add water until it's moldable.
2. Preheat oven to 350° F.
3. Grease the bread pan. Press the mixture into the bread pan to form it into the shape of a loaf.
4. Place the pan in the oven and bake the loaf for 45 minutes.
5. Remove the pan from the oven and let the loaf cool for 15 minutes. Remove the loaf from the pan and let it finish cooling on a wire rack.

Storage:

The seed and nut loaf can be stored at room temperature for a few days before it needs to be refrigerated. It can be stored in the fridge for a week or two or stored in the freezer in an airtight container for a month or two.

Pizza Crust

In my pre-Paleo days, pizza used to be one of my weaknesses. I had a tough time resisting a good slice of pizza . . . or two . . . or three.

When I went Paleo, I thought pizza was a thing of the past. Boy, was I wrong. Paleo-style pizza is even better than regular pizza because you're using fresh, wholesome ingredients to make a delicious pizza that's as guilt-free as pizza can get. You haven't tried pizza until you've had pizza with fresh tomato sauce and homemade nitrate-free meats.

This recipe makes one medium thick-crusted pizza or a couple smaller thin-crusted pizzas. Don't try to roll it out too thin or the crust will become too weak to support any toppings.

Yield: 1 to 2 crusts

Pan Size: Baking tray or pizza stone

Prep Time: 15 minutes

Cook Time: 10 to 15 minutes

Ingredients:

3 eggs.

2 cups almond flour.

¾ cup arrowroot powder.

½ cup almond milk.

1 teaspoon baking powder.

1 teaspoon oregano.

½ teaspoon cumin seeds.

1 ½ teaspoons sea salt.

A pinch of black pepper.

Directions:

1. Combine the almond flour, arrowroot powder, baking powder, oregano, sea salt and black pepper in a bowl.
2. Combine the rest of the ingredients in a separate bowl.
3. Combine the contents of the two bowls.
4. Preheat the oven to 350° F.
5. Spread the dough out onto a greased pizza stone or baking tray. Make sure it's evenly distributed and as close to round as you can get it.
6. Bake the dough for 10 to 15 minutes or until it firms up and starts to lightly brown.
7. Remove from the oven and let cool.

Storage:

This pizza can be stored in the freezer until you're ready to use it. Store it in an airtight container.

Sandwich Bread

I've intentionally avoided using yeast in most of the recipes in this book because there are some Paleo dieters who won't use it. This recipe does include yeast, so if you're one of those people, this recipe isn't for you. I've tried making it a variety of ways without the yeast and it just doesn't turn out the same. The yeast helps it rise and creates an airy loaf, which is perfect for sandwich bread.

Yield: 1 loaf
Pan Size: 9 x 5 bread pan
Prep Time: 2 hours
Cook Time: 50 to 60 minutes

Ingredients:

4 eggs.

2 cups warm water.

1 ½ cups tapioca flour.

1 cup arrowroot powder.

1 cup ground flaxseed.

¾ cup coconut flour.

½ cup ground sunflower seeds.

¼ cup coconut oil.

1 tablespoon honey.

1 tablespoon apple cider vinegar.

2 teaspoons dry active yeast.

1 teaspoon sea salt.

Directions:

1. Warm the water up to around 115° F. The temperature is critical because too hot or cold of water will negatively impact the yeast and in turn will affect the quality of the finished bread.
2. Add the yeast to the water. Let it sit for 10 to 15 minutes.
3. Melt the coconut oil, if it isn't already melted. Add the coconut oil, honey and apple cider vinegar to the yeast water and stir it together. Let it sit for 5 minutes.
4. Combine the rest of the ingredients in a separate bowl.
5. Combine the contents of the two bowls and knead them together. Once you have kneaded dough, cover the bowl with a towel or cloth and let it sit in a warm area of the house for 45 minutes.
6. Press the dough into a greased bread pan and let it rise for an additional hour.
7. Preheat the oven to 350° F.
8. Bake the bread for 50 to 60 minutes or until the top is golden brown. A toothpick inserted into the middle of the bread should come out clean.
9. Let the bread cool for 15 minutes before removing it from the pan. Let it finish cooling on a wire rack.

Storage:

This bread can be stored in the fridge for a few days. It can be stored for a month or two in an airtight container in the freezer.

Rolls and Muffins

In this chapter, you'll find all sorts of rolls and muffins. We've got all the meals covered, from breakfast to dinner and even dessert. If you thought muffins and rolls were a thing of the past when you went gluten-free, this chapter will show you how to add healthy gluten-free varieties back into your diet.

Most of the recipes in this section can be adjusted to fit your personal tastes. An example of this is the peach muffins near the end of the chapter. They could just as easily be made with berries, apricots, pears or any number of other fruits. Don't be afraid to experiment. Some of my best recipes have come about because I thought something along the lines of, "I wonder what would happen if I used…"

Blueberry Breakfast Rolls

I love a good breakfast roll. This recipe is one of my go-to breakfast roll recipes. The cinnamon and raisins are optional and can be subbed for blueberries, apricot preserves or any number of other fruits or fruit preserves.

Yield: 1 loaf

Pan Size: Baking sheet.

Prep Time: 10 minutes

Cook Time: 30 to 40 minutes

Ingredients:

1 egg.

1 cup potato or tapioca starch.

½ cup water.

¼ cup coconut flour.

½ cup melted coconut oil.

3 tablespoons honey.

½ teaspoon sea salt.

1 teaspoon cinnamon.

Raisins, to taste.

Directions:

1. Beat the egg. Add the water, honey and coconut oil and beat them into the egg.

2. Add the potato starch, cinnamon, coconut flour and sea salt to the bowl and mix them in. If the dough is too runny, add ½ a teaspoon of coconut flour at a time and stir it in until the dough is moldable.
3. Fold the raisins into the dough.
4. Preheat the oven to 350° F.
5. Line a baking sheet with parchment paper.
6. Roll the dough into 8 to 10 balls and place the balls on the baking sheet.
7. Bake for 30 to 40 minutes or until the rolls are golden brown.
8. Let the rolls cool for 15 minutes after they come out of the oven.

Storage:

These rolls can be stored at room temperature for a couple days. They can be stored in the fridge or the freezer, but will need to be reheated prior to consumption to soften them up a bit.

Banana Bread Breakfast Muffins

I recently had a potluck at work and was asked to bring dessert. A couple of friends jokingly told me not to bring something Paleo because they'd tried Paleo desserts before and they were dry and bland. I made this recipe and didn't tell them the muffins they were stuffing in their face were Paleo until after they'd gone back for seconds.

If you've got a chocolate craving, try adding chunks of dark chocolate to this recipe. Just make sure you get pure dark chocolate that isn't made in a facility where it can be cross-contaminated with gluten. Dark chocolate is about as close to being Paleo as chocolate gets. It's up to you whether you want to "fudge" the rules a little.

Yield: 12 muffins

Pan Size: 12-cup muffin tin

Prep Time: 20 minutes

Cook Time: 20 to 30 minutes

Ingredients:

½ cup coconut flour.

7 eggs.

1 large ripe banana.

½ cup coconut milk.

¼ cup coconut oil.

½ teaspoon baking soda.

½ teaspoon salt.

OPTIONAL: 1 teaspoon pure vanilla extract.

OPTIONAL: Dark chocolate chunks.

Directions:

1. Combine the eggs, coconut milk and coconut oil in a bowl.
2. Mash the banana and beat it into the contents of the bowl.
3. Stir in the rest of the ingredients.
4. Preheat the oven to 350° F.
5. Line 12 wells in a muffin tin with cupcake liners.
6. Divide the batter amongst the wells.
7. Place the muffin tin in the oven and cook the muffins for 20 to 30 minutes or until the muffins are golden brown on top.
8. Let the muffins cool in the tin for 10 minutes. Transfer them to a wire cooling rack and let them cool for an additional 15 minutes before eating or prepping for storage.

Storage:

These muffins should be stored in an airtight container in the fridge or freezer. They'll last up to a week in the fridge and a month or two in the freezer.

Dinner Rolls

The perfect dinner roll is soft and moist on the inside with a crisp outer shell. It's a tough combination to achieve using only Paleo-friendly ingredients. This recipe hits the mark by making use of potato starch to make what I think is the perfect Paleo dinner roll.

If you include dairy in your diet, try making these rolls with ½ cup melted butter instead of the olive oil. It adds a buttery flavor to the rolls that makes them irresistible.

Yield: 8 to 10 rolls
Pan Size: Baking sheet
Prep Time: 10 minutes
Cook Time: 30 to 40 minutes

Ingredients:

1 egg.

1 cup potato starch.

½ cup water.

¼ cup coconut flour.

½ cup extra virgin olive oil.

1 teaspoon sea salt.

Directions:

1. Beat the egg. Add the water and olive oil and beat them into the egg.

2. Add the potato starch, coconut flour and sea salt to the bowl and mix them in. If the dough is too runny, add ½ a teaspoon of coconut powder at a time and stir it in until the dough is moldable.
3. Preheat the oven to 350° F.
4. Grease a baking sheet or line it with parchment paper.
5. Roll the dough into 8 to 10 balls and place the balls on the baking sheet.
6. Bake for 30 to 40 minutes or until the rolls are golden brown.
7. Let the rolls cool for 15 minutes before serving.

Storage:

These rolls can be stored at room temperature for a couple days. They can be stored in the fridge or the freezer, but will need to be reheated prior to consumption to soften them up a bit.

Microwave Coconut Flour Muffins

I had trouble deciding what exactly to call these.

They're kind of a cross between muffins and buns. They're light and airy enough to be muffins, yet they remind me of hamburger buns. Call them whatever you want; they're great for breakfast sandwiches and are a decent snack on their own with honey drizzled over them.

These muffins are made in the microwave, so they're quick and easy to make when you need a bread fix, but don't have time to whip up bread that has to be cooked in the oven.

Yield: 2 muffins

Pan Size: Coffee mug

Prep Time: 5 minutes

Cook Time: 75 seconds

Ingredients:

1 egg.

2 tablespoons coconut milk.

1 tablespoon coconut flour.

1 teaspoon extra virgin olive oil.

½ teaspoon baking powder.

A pinch of sea salt.

Directions:

1. Place the coconut flour, baking powder and sea salt into a bowl and mix them together.
2. Fold the egg, coconut milk and olive oil into the dry ingredients and stir until incorporated.
3. Grease 2 coffee mugs with vegetable oil and divide the batter between the mugs.
4. Let the contents of the mugs settle for a couple minutes.
5. Microwave each mug for 60 to 75 seconds, or until the muffins are cooked all the way through.
6. Let the muffins cool for 5 minutes before removing them from the mug. The easiest way to do this is to run a thin blade or another flat object around the edge of the mug to break the muffin free.
7. Slice the muffin in half and gently toast it before making a sandwich or eating it with honey or jam.

Storage:

These muffins don't store well and are best if eaten within a few hours of cooking them.

Peach Muffins

These muffins have delectable little bits of peach in every bite. Fresh peaches work best, but you can use thawed frozen peaches if that's all you have. I've also made it with peach preserves and it turned out well. If you use preserves, you can eliminate some of the honey.

Yield: 8 to 10 muffins

Pan Size: Muffin tin

Prep Time: 15 minutes

Cook Time: 20 to 30 minutes

Ingredients:

3 eggs.

1 ½ cups peaches, peeled and diced.

2 cups almond flour.

4 tablespoons raw honey.

2 tablespoons melted coconut oil.

2 tablespoons fresh lemon juice.

1 teaspoon vanilla extract.

½ teaspoon baking soda.

½ teaspoon cinnamon.

A dash of sea salt.

Directions:

1. Combine the eggs, honey, lemon juice, vanilla and coconut oil in a bowl.
2. Add the almond flour, baking soda, cinnamon and sea salt and stir it in.
3. Fold the peaches into the batter.
4. Preheat the oven to 350° F.
5. Line 10 wells in a muffin tin with cupcake liners.
6. Divide the batter amongst the wells.
7. Place the muffin tin in the oven and cook for 20 to 30 minutes or until the muffins are golden brown on top and a toothpick inserted into the center of the muffins comes out clean.
8. Let the muffins cool in the tin for 10 minutes. Transfer them to a wire cooling rack and let them cool for an additional 15 minutes before eating or prepping for storage.

Storage:

These muffins should be stored in an airtight container in the fridge or freezer. They'll last up to a week in the fridge and a month or two in the freezer.

Strawberry Muffins

I live in a warm climate, so I'm lucky enough to have a long growing season for strawberries. I love strawberries and can't pass up a good deal on them. At times, I find myself with strawberries that are right on the verge of going bad. They aren't ideal for eating, but they work well in recipes like this one that integrate strawberries into baked goods.

There's nothing better than the smell of these strawberry muffins creeping through the house as they bake. Since I'm always the one cooking them, I don't know what it's like to wake up to the delicious smell of fresh strawberry muffins, but I know I never have any problems getting the kids out of bed when I've got them in the oven.

If you want buttery muffins and aren't on a strict Paleo diet that disallows dairy, try subbing butter for the coconut oil.

Yield: 8 to 10 muffins

Pan Size: Muffin tin

Prep Time: 20 minutes

Cook Time: 20 to 30 minutes

Ingredients:

4 eggs.

1 ½ cups strawberries, stemmed and cut into small chunks.

2 ½ cups almond flour.

¼ cup raw honey.

3 tablespoons melted coconut oil.

2 tablespoons fresh lemon juice.

1 teaspoon vanilla extract.

½ teaspoon baking soda.

¼ teaspoon sea salt.

Directions:

1. Combine the eggs, honey, lemon juice, vanilla and coconut oil in a bowl.
2. Add the almond flour, baking soda and sea salt and stir it in.
3. Fold the strawberries into the batter.
4. Preheat the oven to 350° F.
5. Line 10 wells in a muffin tin with cupcake liners.
6. Divide the batter amongst the wells.
7. Place the muffin tin in the oven and cook for 20 to 30 minutes or until the muffins are golden brown on top and a toothpick inserted into the center of the muffins comes out clean.
8. Let the muffins cool in the tin for 10 minutes. Transfer them to a wire cooling rack and let them cool for an additional 15 minutes before eating or prepping for storage.

Storage:

These muffins should be stored in an airtight container in the fridge or freezer. They'll last up to a week in the fridge and a month or two in the freezer.

Tapioca Flour Dinner Rolls

Tapioca flour is made from a root vegetable that's native to Brazil. It's one of the closest matches to grain-based flour there is, but you don't get much nutritional value from it. It is gluten-free, so it can be used by those on a gluten-free diet to create baked goods that are light and fluffy.

Tapioca flour dinner rolls aren't too far removed from your average dinner roll, minus the gluten. They can be served as a side dish or you can cut them in half and make burgers or sandwiches.

Yield: 24 rolls

Pan Size: Baking tray

Prep Time: 15 minutes

Cook Time: 30 to 40 minutes

Ingredients:

2 cups tapioca flour.

½ cup coconut flour.

1 cup water.

1 cup extra virgin olive oil.

2 eggs.

2 teaspoons sea salt.

Directions:

1. Combine the tapioca flour, coconut flour and sea salt in a bowl.
2. Whisk the eggs in a separate bowl. Add the water and olive oil to the eggs and whisk them in.
3. Combine the contents of both bowls and stir them together. Once combined, you should have slightly sticky dough that can be molded into balls that'll hold their shape. If the dough is too runny, add a tablespoon or two of coconut flour.
4. Preheat the oven to 350° F.
5. Roll the dough into equal-sized balls and place them on a baking pan greased with coconut oil. You'll have approximately 24 rolls, so you'll need two baking pans.
6. Bake for 30 to 40 minutes or until the rolls are golden brown and cooked all the way through.
7. Transfer the rolls to a wire rack to cool.

Storage:

These rolls can be stored at room temperature for a day or two before they start to dry out. Store them in an airtight container in the fridge for up to 5 days or in the freezer for up to a month.

Additional Reading

I hope you enjoy making the recipes in this book as much as I have. If you're interested in further reading on the Paleo diet, here's a link to another of my books:

http://www.amazon.com/Paleo-Probiotics-Fermented-Foods-Living-ebook/dp/B00GYI4F08/

Printed in Great Britain
by Amazon.co.uk, Ltd.,
Marston Gate.